J
975.7
MCA   McAuliffe, Bill

        South Carolina
        facts and symbols

                WITHDRAWN

                ON LINE

MORRIS AUTOMATED INFORMATION NETWORK

0 1014 0072991 5   JUL   1999

JEFFERSON TWP PUBLIC LIBRARY
1031 WELDON RD
OAK RIDGE, NJ 07438-9511
(973) 208-6115

DEMCO

South Carolina
Facts and Symbols

by Bill McAuliffe

Jefferson Twp. Public Library
1031 Weldon Road
Oak Ridge, NJ 07438
(973) 208-6115

Consultant:
Michael J. Berson, Ph.D.
Past President
South Carolina Council for the Social Studies

Hilltop Books
an imprint of Franklin Watts
A Division of Grolier Publishing
New York   London   Hong Kong   Sydney
Danbury, Connecticut

Hilltop Books
http://publishing.grolier.com

Copyright © 1999 by Capstone Press. All rights reserved.
No part of this book may be reproduced without written permission from
the publisher. The publisher takes no responsibility for the use of any of
the materials or methods described in this book, nor for the products thereof.
Printed in the United States of America. Published simultaneously in Canada.

Library of Congress Cataloging-in-Publication Data
McAuliffe, Bill.
    South Carolina facts and symbols/by Bill McAuliffe.
    p. cm.—(The states and their symbols)
    Includes bibliographical references (p. 23) and index.
    Summary: Presents information about the state of South Carolina, its nickname, motto, and
emblems.
    ISBN 0-7368-0220-7
    1. Emblems, State—South Carolina—Juvenile literature. [1. Emblems, State—South
Carolina. 2. South Carolina.] I. Title. II. Series: McAuliffe, Emily. States and their symbols.
CR203.S6M38   1999
975.7—dc21   98-43013
                                                                                                        CIP
                                                                                                        AC

Editorial Credits
Blanche R. Bolland, editor; Steve Christensen, cover designer; Linda Clavel, illustrator;
    Kimberly Danger and Sheri Gosewisch, photo researchers

Photo Credits
Cole Photo/Fred Whitehead, cover
Corbis-Bettmann, 6
Henry Aldrich, 16
John Elk II, 10, 22 (middle)
Karen McClymonds, 22 (top)
Lee Kline, 18
One Mile Up, Inc., 8, 10 (inset)
PhotoBank, Inc./James Lafayette, 22 (bottom)
Transparencies, Inc./Robert Clark, 20
Visuals Unlimited/Maslowski, 12
William B. Folsom, 14

Table of Contents

North Carolina

Blue Ridge Mountains

SOUTH CAROLINA

Pee Dee River

★ Columbia

Congaree Swamp
National Monument

Georgia

Charleston ●
Fort Sumter ▥

Atlantic Ocean

▥ Hilton Head Island

○ City
✪ Capital
〰 River
▲ Mountains
▥ Places to
  Visit

Fast Facts

Capital: Columbia is the capital of South Carolina.
Largest City: Columbia is the largest city in South Carolina. More than 104,000 people live in Columbia.
Size: South Carolina covers 31,113 square miles (80,583 square kilometers). It ranks 40th of the 50 states in size.
Location: South Carolina is in the southeastern United States. This state lies on the Atlantic Ocean.
Population: About 3,760,181 people live in South Carolina (U.S. Census Bureau, 1997 estimate).
Statehood: South Carolina became the eighth state on May 23, 1788.
Natural Resources: South Carolina's natural resources include forest products, kaolin, limestone, and fish.
Manufactured Goods: Workers in South Carolina make dyes, cloth, paper products, and machinery.
Crops: Farmers in South Carolina grow tobacco, soybeans, and peaches. They also raise cattle, hogs, and chickens.

State Name and Nickname

South Carolina was named after a king of England. Charles I gave land in America to Sir Robert Heath in 1629. The land was a gift for helping Charles I become king. Part of this land became South Carolina. The name first was spelled Carolana. This means Land of Charles in Latin.

South Carolina's nickname is the Palmetto State. The state earned its nickname during the Revolutionary War (1775–1783). The 13 American colonies fought for freedom from Great Britain during that war.

South Carolina soldiers won a famous battle in 1776. They fought from a palmetto log fort on Sullivans Island. They fired at 11 British ships in Charleston's harbor. The ships caught fire. The soldiers thought the smoke above the ships looked like a palmetto tree.

South Carolina was named for Charles I. He was king of England from 1625 to 1649.

State Seal and Motto

South Carolina adopted its state seal in 1776. The state seal reminds South Carolinians of their state's government. The seal also makes government papers official.

South Carolina's state seal shows a palmetto tree. The palmetto stands above a dead oak tree. These trees represent the battle on Sullivans Island in 1776. The palmetto stands for the South Carolina fort. The oak stands for the British ship.

The seal also shows a woman on a beach. The woman represents hope. Swords cover the beach. These weapons stand for danger. The picture means hope can beat danger.

South Carolinians adopted two state mottoes in 1776. Both mottoes are in Latin. One motto means Prepared in Mind and Resources. The other means While I Breathe, I Hope. These sayings announce South Carolinians' strength and hope.

The laurel branches on the state seal stand for the victory on Sullivans Island.

State Capitol and Flag

The state capitol building is in Columbia. Columbia is South Carolina's capital city. Government officials meet in the capitol to make the state's laws.

Workers began building the capitol in 1851. But officials kept changing the building's plans. Then the Civil War (1861–1865) began between Northern and Southern states. Work on the capitol stopped. Builders finally finished the capitol in 1904. The building cost about $3.5 million.

Officials adopted the state flag in 1861. The flag is blue with a silver crescent and a palmetto tree. The flag honors South Carolina soldiers who fought in the Revolutionary War. Blue was the color of their uniforms. The moon shape is like the symbol on the soldiers' hats. The palmetto tree stands for the Sullivans Island battle in 1776.

South Carolina's state capitol is in Columbia.

State Bird and Game Bird

The Carolina wren became the state bird in 1948. This bird lives in all areas of South Carolina. The Carolina wren measures about 5 inches (13 centimeters) long.

Carolina wrens have brown backs and wings. Their breast feathers are tan. These colors become brighter in cooler weather. Carolina wrens have a white stripe above their eyes.

South Carolina also has a state game bird. People can hunt game birds. South Carolina's game bird is the wild turkey.

The wild turkey is North America's largest game bird. Males can grow up to 46 inches (117 centimeters) long. They weigh between 15 and 28 pounds (7 and 13 kilograms).

Wild turkeys have a long neck that is red in the front. They have a floppy piece of skin at their throat called a wattle.

Carolina wrens often build nests in containers.

State Tree

The palmetto became South Carolina's state tree in 1939. Swamp cabbage and sabal palm are other names for the palmetto. The palmetto grows in the southeastern United States. It measures about 30 feet (9 meters) tall. The trunk has rough, gray-brown bark.

Palmetto leaves are about 4 to 7 feet (1 to 2 meters) long. The leaves are on a long stalk. They spread like fans and droop at the ends. It takes many years for new leaves to form.

Early settlers used all parts of the palmetto tree. They ate the buds. Settlers built the walls of their houses from the trunks. They covered the roofs with palmetto leaves.

Today, the palmetto still has uses. People build docks with the wood. They eat the inner part of the leaf buds. Some people use these hearts of palm in salads.

Palmetto leaves grow on long stalks.

State Flower

The yellow jessamine is South Carolina's state flower. Government officials chose this flower in 1924 for several reasons. The yellow jessamine is native to every part of South Carolina. South Carolinians say its color suggests the pureness of gold.

The yellow jessamine is a vine. Its leaves stay green all year. The vines cover trees and fences in South Carolina. The jessamine often grows near pine trees.

The yellow jessamine is one of the first flowers to bloom in spring. It has many yellow blossoms shaped like trumpets. Each blossom is about 1 inch (2.5 centimeters) long. The blossoms have a sweet smell.

All parts of the yellow jessamine are poisonous. People and animals will get sick if they eat this plant.

The yellow jessamine is a vine. It is one of the first flowers to bloom in spring.

State Animal

The white-tailed deer became South Carolina's state animal in 1972. The tails of these deer are brown on top and white underneath. White-tailed deer hold up their tails when they run. These deer also raise their tails when they sense danger. This flash of white warns other deer.

White-tailed deer live throughout the United States and southern Canada. These deer live in wooded areas. But they often come into open fields for food. People see deer most often around sunrise and sunset. Deer feed at these times.

Male deer measure up to 6 feet (180 centimeters) long. They weigh about 200 pounds (91 kilograms).

Male deer have antlers. Males lose these branched horns every winter. When the antlers grow back, they sometimes have more branches.

White-tailed deer can run fast. They can jump far and high.

More State Symbols

State Dog: A South Carolina hunter bred the first Boykin spaniel about 90 years ago. The Boykin spaniel became the state dog in 1985.

State Fish: In 1972, South Carolinians chose the striped bass as the state fish. The striped bass lives in the Atlantic Ocean.

State Gem: The amethyst became South Carolina's state gem in 1969. This valuable stone is purple or violet. South Carolina is one of three states that has high-quality amethyst.

State Reptile: The loggerhead sea turtle has been the state reptile since 1988. This turtle can weigh as much as 1,000 pounds (454 kilograms). It sometimes travels thousands of miles to eat and nest.

State Song: South Carolina has two state songs. "Carolina" became the first state song in 1911. South Carolinians chose "South Carolina on My Mind" as their second state song in 1984.

Boykin spaniels make good pets and hunting dogs.

Places to Visit

Congaree Swamp National Monument

The Congaree Swamp became part of the National Park System in 1976. The Congaree is one of the last remaining large swamps. Visitors can explore this park by foot or canoe. About 40 kinds of mammals live there. They include wild pigs, bobcats, and flying squirrels.

Fort Sumter National Monument

Fort Sumter National Monument sits on Sullivans Island in Charleston Harbor. This military base includes both Fort Sumter and Fort Moultrie. Soldiers at these two forts defended the seacoast for 171 years. Visitors can see displays and films. They also can take tours on foot or by boat.

Hilton Head Island

Hilton Head is the second-largest U.S. barrier island. This long, sandy island protects the South Carolina coast from the ocean. Hilton Head Island has many beaches and resorts. Visitors play tennis and golf, take nature walks, and go boating. Special boat trips to watch for dolphins are popular.

Words to Know

antlers (ANT-lurs)—horns that grow in branches

barrier island (BA-ree-ur EYE-luhnd)—a long, sandy island that is built up by the action of waves, currents, and winds; a barrier island protects the shore from the ocean.

crescent (KRESS-uhnt)—a curved shape like the moon when it is just a sliver in the sky

fort (FORT)—a building that is strongly built to survive attacks

Latin (LAT-uhn)—the language of the ancient Romans

motto (MOT-oh)—a word or saying people believe in

sword (SORD)—a weapon with a handle and a long, sharp blade

wattle (WOT-uhl)—wrinkled skin that hangs from the chin or throat of a bird or reptile

Read More

Capstone Press Geography Department. *South Carolina.* One Nation. Mankato, Minn.: Capstone Press, 1997.

Krull, Kathleen. *Bridges to Change: How Kids Live on a South Carolina Sea Island.* A World of My Own. New York: Lodestar Books, 1995.

Thompson, Kathleen. *South Carolina.* Portrait of America. Austin, Texas: Raintree Steck-Vaughn, 1996.

Useful Addresses

South Carolina Department of Archives and History
P.O. Box 11669
1430 Senate Street
Columbia, SC 29211

South Carolina Division of Tourism
P.O. Box 71
Columbia, SC 29202

Internet Sites

South Carolina
http://www.travelsc.com/welcome/index.html
South Carolina General Assembly Kids' Page
http://www.lpitr.state.sc.us/kids.htm
South Carolina History
http://www.state.sc.us/histro.html

Index